Harnessing the Power of the DISC Framework for Effective Communication,

Dealing with Difficult (Different) Employees

Glenn E DGnGelG

Table Of Contents

Introduction to DISC:

The DISC assessment is a powerful tool allowing individuals to deeply understand human behavior and communication styles. By exploring the four key dimensions: Dominance, Influence, Steadiness, and Compliance, the DISC model provides valuable insights into how people interact with others and approach tasks. Developed in the 1920s by psychologist William Moulton Marston, this framework continues to be widely used and embraced for its comprehensive understanding of human behavior.

Definition and Origin:

DISC is an acronym for Dominance, Influence, Steadiness, and Compliance. These four dimensions represent distinct behavioral styles that individuals exhibit to varying degrees. The Dominance dimension reflects assertiveness, decisiveness, and a purposeful approach. The Influence dimension embodies outgoingness, enthusiasm, and persuasiveness. Steadiness represents calmness, reliability, and collaborative tendencies, while compliance signifies attention to detail, systematic thinking, and an emphasis on accuracy.

William Moulton Marston, a renowned psychologist known for his emotional work, developed DISC in the 1920s. He focused his research on human emotions and their impact on behavior. Marston believed that understanding these behavioral styles would enhance comprehension of self-awareness and interpersonal relationships.

Purpose of DISC:

The DISC assessment's primary purpose is to gain insight into human behavior patterns and enhance self-awareness to improve interpersonal relationships. By exploring the four dimensions provided by the DISC model—Dominance (D), Influence (I), Steadiness (S), and Compliance (C)—individuals can develop a shared language to discuss their behavioral tendencies. Understanding one's style through DISC can be beneficial in both personal and professional settings. It allows individuals to identify their strengths and weaknesses in communication, teamwork, and collaboration. With this knowledge, individuals can enhance their emotional intelligence, conflict resolution skills, and overall effectiveness in building relationships.

DISC assessments can be used in work environments for staff development, ensuring effective engagement and fostering a cohesive team dynamic. Organizations can also leverage DISC to make informed hiring decisions by matching candidates' behavioral styles with job requirements.

The goal is to foster an environment that promotes effective communication and nurtures confident leaders who understand their impact on others. By delving into the intricacies of the DISC assessment and its application in contexts such as customer service or sales skills training programs, organizations can harness data-driven insights to develop impactful leaders and cultivate a culture of collaboration and effective communication.

The comprehensive nature of the DISC profiles equips individuals with a deep understanding of themselves, offering valuable insights into others' behavioral tendencies. By using DISC as a tool for personal growth, individuals pave the way for enhanced self-awareness and improved relationships in both personal and professional spheres.

The Four Dimensions of DISC:
Dominance (D):
Dominance, one of the four dimensions in the DISC model, is characterized by assertive, decisive, and results-oriented individuals. Those with a dominant communication style tend to be straightforward, focusing on outcomes rather than nuances.

They excel in leadership roles, being natural leaders, problem solvers, and decision-makers. Their ability to take charge and make critical decisions can significantly influence an organization's success. However, dominance can sometimes be perceived as aggressive or impatient.

Influence (I):
Influence, another dimension within the DISC framework, encompasses outgoing, enthusiastic, and persuasive individuals. People with influential communication styles possess outstanding social skills; they are talkative, expressive, and highly people-centric. They excel at motivating others, functioning well in teams, and easily building relationships.

Their optimism can drive projects forward, but they might sometimes overlook details due to impulsiveness.

Steadiness (S):

Steadiness features individuals who exhibit calmness, reservation, and predictability within the DISC model. Those with a steady communication style excel in attentive listening and offering collaborative support. They prioritize harmony in relationships and aim to provide stability. They are known for their loyalty and ability to foster cohesive teams. However, their aversion to conflicts or change might hinder their adaptability.

Compliance (C):

Compliance, the final dimension of DISC, characterizes individuals who are systematic, meticulous, and persistent. Those with a compliant communication style prioritize factual and respectful discussions, focusing on precision and accuracy. They thrive as meticulous planners and researchers, ensuring thorough examination of all project aspects. Their strength lies in making data-driven decisions and contributing to effective problem-solving processes. However, they might occasionally become overly perfectionistic or critical.

A Thought:

Incorporating the DISC model into our understanding of human behavior and communication styles provides invaluable personal and professional growth insights. Recognizing the diverse dimensions of dominance, Influence, steadiness, and compliance can foster effective engagement, enhance teamwork, and nurture confident leaders. The common language DISC provides facilitates improved conflict resolution skills and better relationships through enhanced communication. By embracing the power of DISC, organizations can build collaborative teams that drive success, positively affecting individual lives inside and outside the workplace.

DISC
Assessment

Instructions: For each statement below, rate yourself on a scale of 1 to 5, where 1 means "Strongly Disagree," and 5 means "Strongly Agree." Be honest with your answers.

Dominance (D)

1. I enjoy taking charge of situations.

2. I am assertive and speak up for what I believe in.

3. I am comfortable making decisions quickly.

4. I thrive in competitive situations.

5. I am driven by results and achieving goals.

6. I prefer to lead rather than follow.

7. I am confident in my ability to solve problems.

Total _____

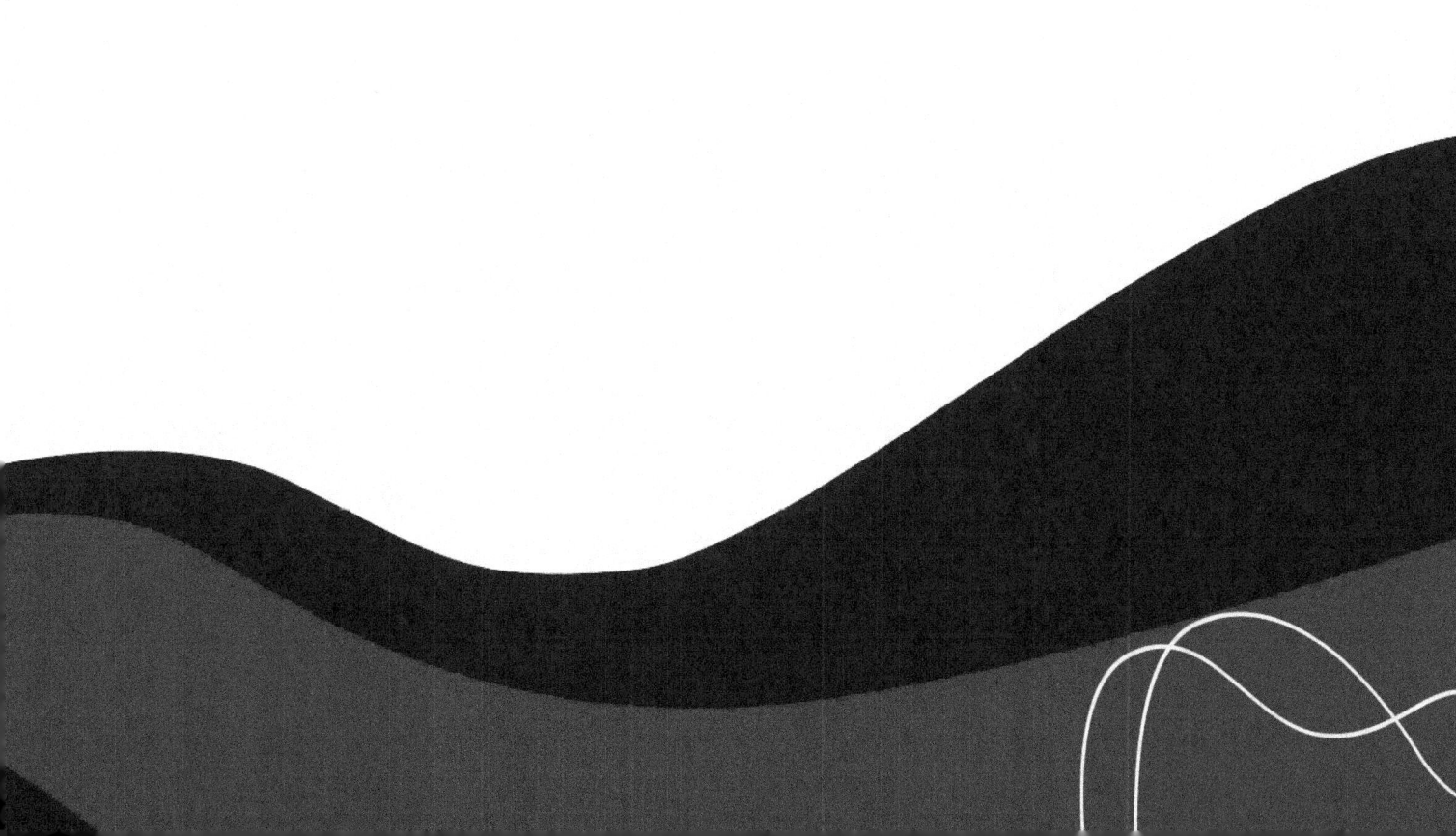

03

Influence
(I)

1. I am enthusiastic and optimistic.
2. I am persuasive and good at influencing others.
3. I am often the life of the party.
4. I value building relationships and networking.
5. I am comfortable expressing my feelings and thoughts.
6. I am often described as charismatic.
7. I am patient and calm in stressful situations.

Total ____

04

Steadiness (S)

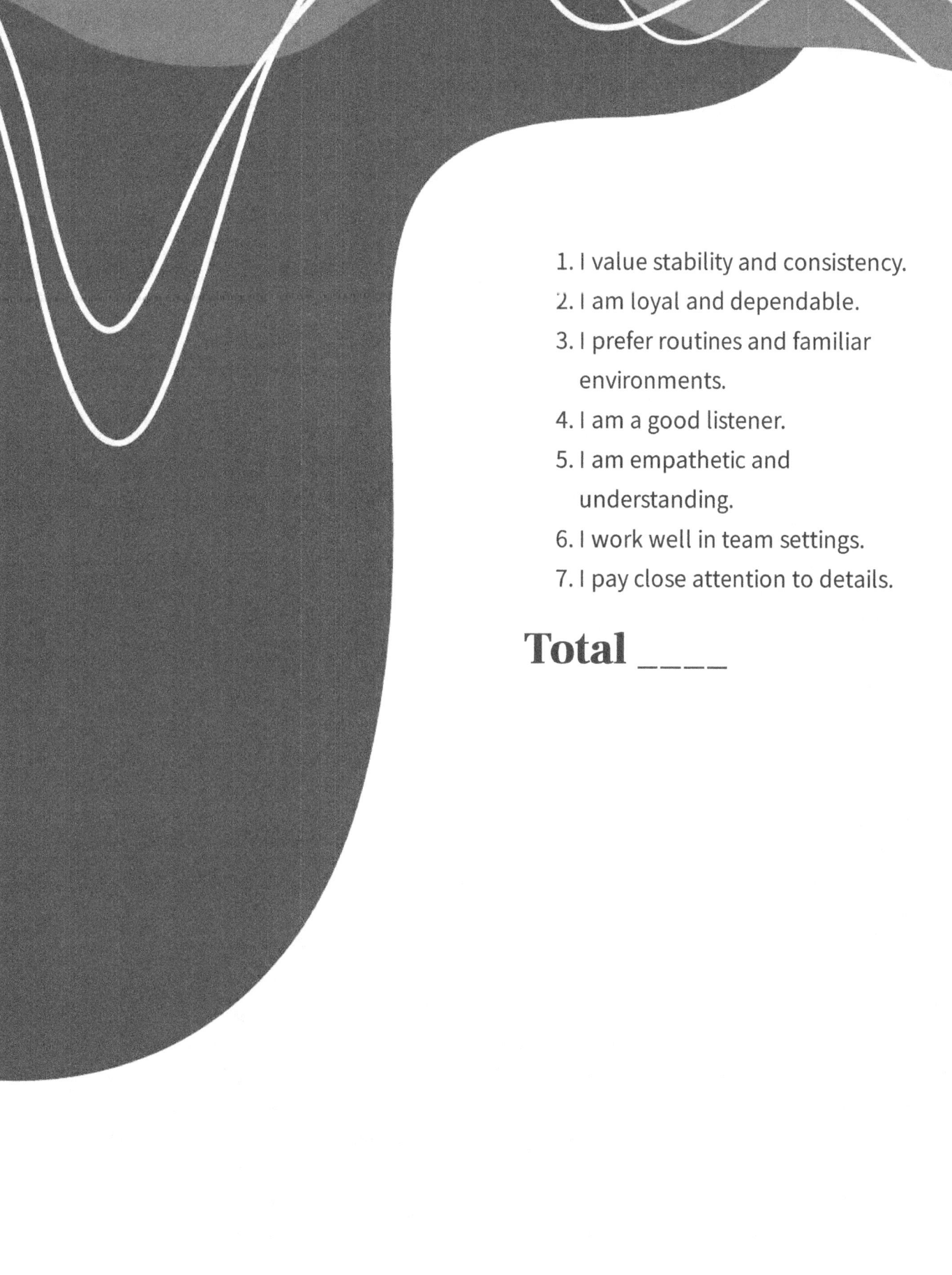

1. I value stability and consistency.
2. I am loyal and dependable.
3. I prefer routines and familiar environments.
4. I am a good listener.
5. I am empathetic and understanding.
6. I work well in team settings.
7. I pay close attention to details.

Total _____

05

Conscientiousness (C)

1. I am organized and systematic.
2. I always strive for accuracy in my work.
3. I follow the rules and guidelines closely.
4. I think things through before making decisions.
5. I value quality over quantity.
6. I am cautious and careful.
7. I prefer to have a plan before taking action.

Total

Scoring & Results

1. Tally up your scores for each section (D, I, S, C).
2. The maximum score for each section is 35, and the minimum is 7.

Dominance (D) _____

Influence (I) _____

Steadiness (S)_____

Conscientiousness (C) _____

07

Interpreting Your
DISC Profile:

- Dominance (D): High scores indicate a preference for leading, making decisions, and taking on challenges. Low scores may suggest a more collaborative or cautious approach.
- Influence (I): High scores suggest you're outgoing, persuasive, and relationship-oriented. Low scores may indicate a more reserved or introspective nature.
- Steadiness (S): High scores indicate patience, consistency, and a preference for stability. Low scores might suggest a preference for variety or change.
- Conscientiousness (C): High scores show a preference for organization, detail, and accuracy. Low scores might indicate a more flexible or spontaneous approach.

08

DISC Personality Types: Delving into Desires, Fears, and Tailored Communication Strategies

The DISC personality assessment is a prominent tool for categorizing individual behavioral tendencies and personality traits. The acronym DISC represents:

- D: Dominance
- I: Influence
- S: Steadiness
- C: Conscientiousness

Let's delve deeper into the desires, fears, and tailored communication strategies for each type, incorporating real-life scenarios for clarity:

09

D
(Dominance)

Desires:

- Autonomy in their surroundings
- Decisive authority in decision-making
- Recognition for personal achievements

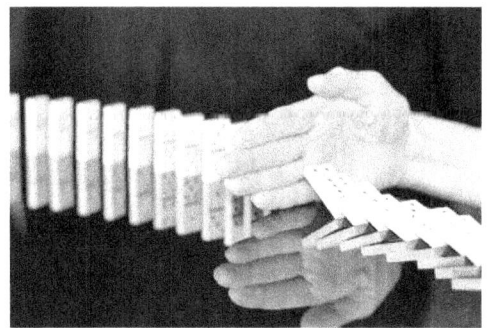

Fears:

- Being seen as susceptible or easily deceived
- Losing their leadership or influence
- Being viewed as ineffective

Communication Strategies:

- Opt for concise and direct communication, avoiding extraneous details.
- Value their achievements and leadership skills.
- Present information logically, anticipating potential challenges.

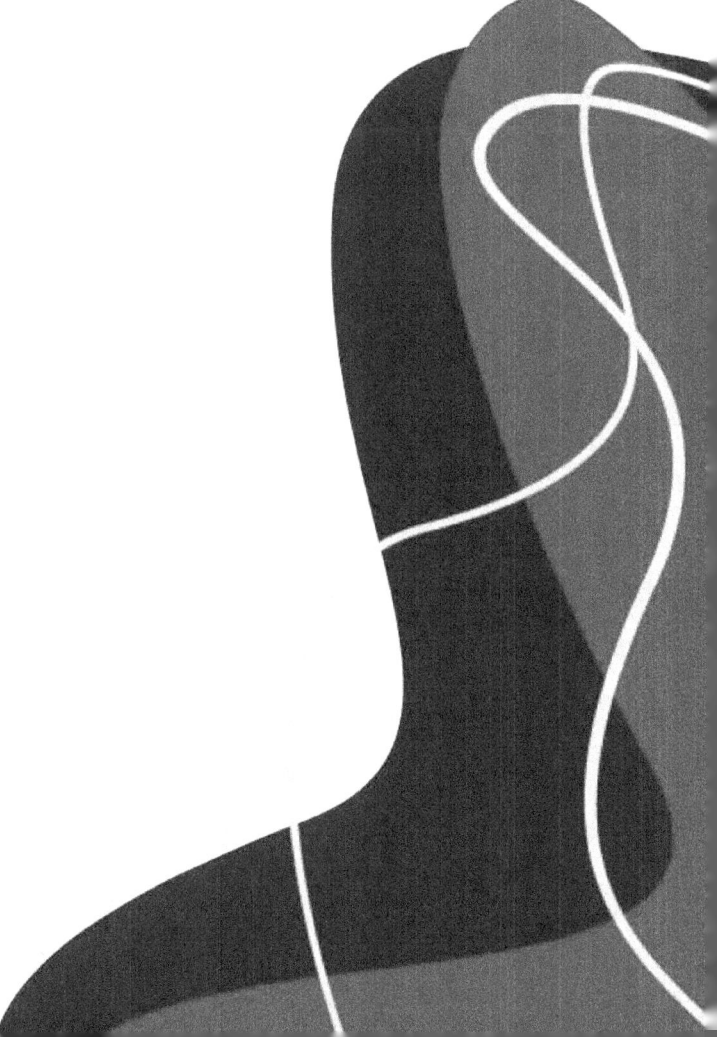

Scenario: Imagine presenting a business proposal to Mark, a "D" personality type. Highlight the project's advantages, especially how it could bolster the company's standing in the market. Mark will likely appreciate a direct approach and swiftly decide on the project's feasibility.

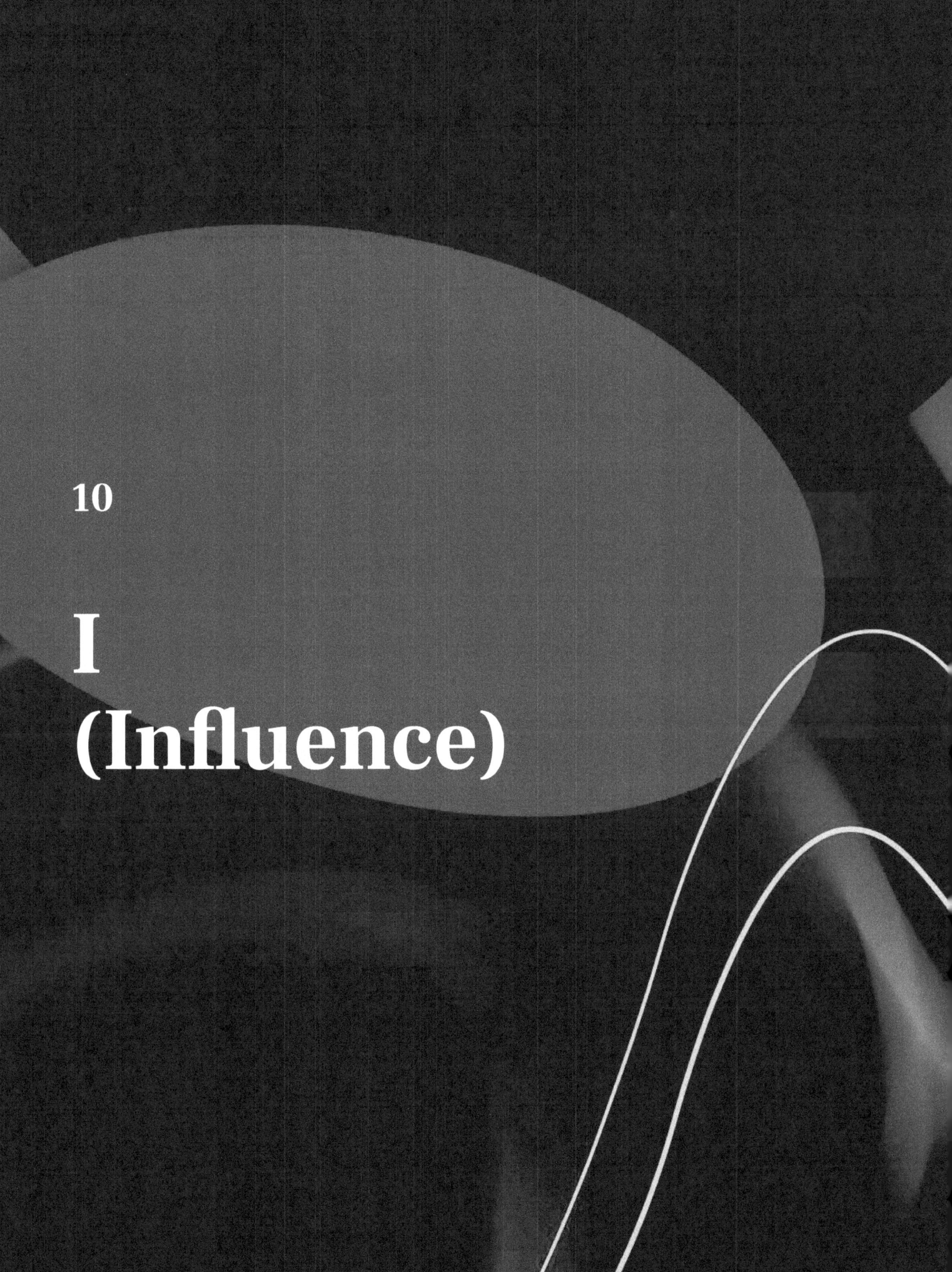

10

I
(Influence)

Desires:

- Affirmation from social circles
- Inclusion in teams or groups
- Opportunities for verbal interactions and influencing peers

Fears:

- Social alienation
- Reduced influence or being overshadowed
- Feeling unacknowledged or overlooked

Communication Strategies:

- Encourage open dialogue, allowing space for their opinions.
- Show genuine enthusiasm and provide positive feedback.
- Actively listen and validate their feelings.

Scenario: Sarah, an "I" type, contributes a new marketing idea during a team meeting. Recognizing her effort publicly and creating a platform to elaborate on her concept would motivate her and strengthen her bond with the team.

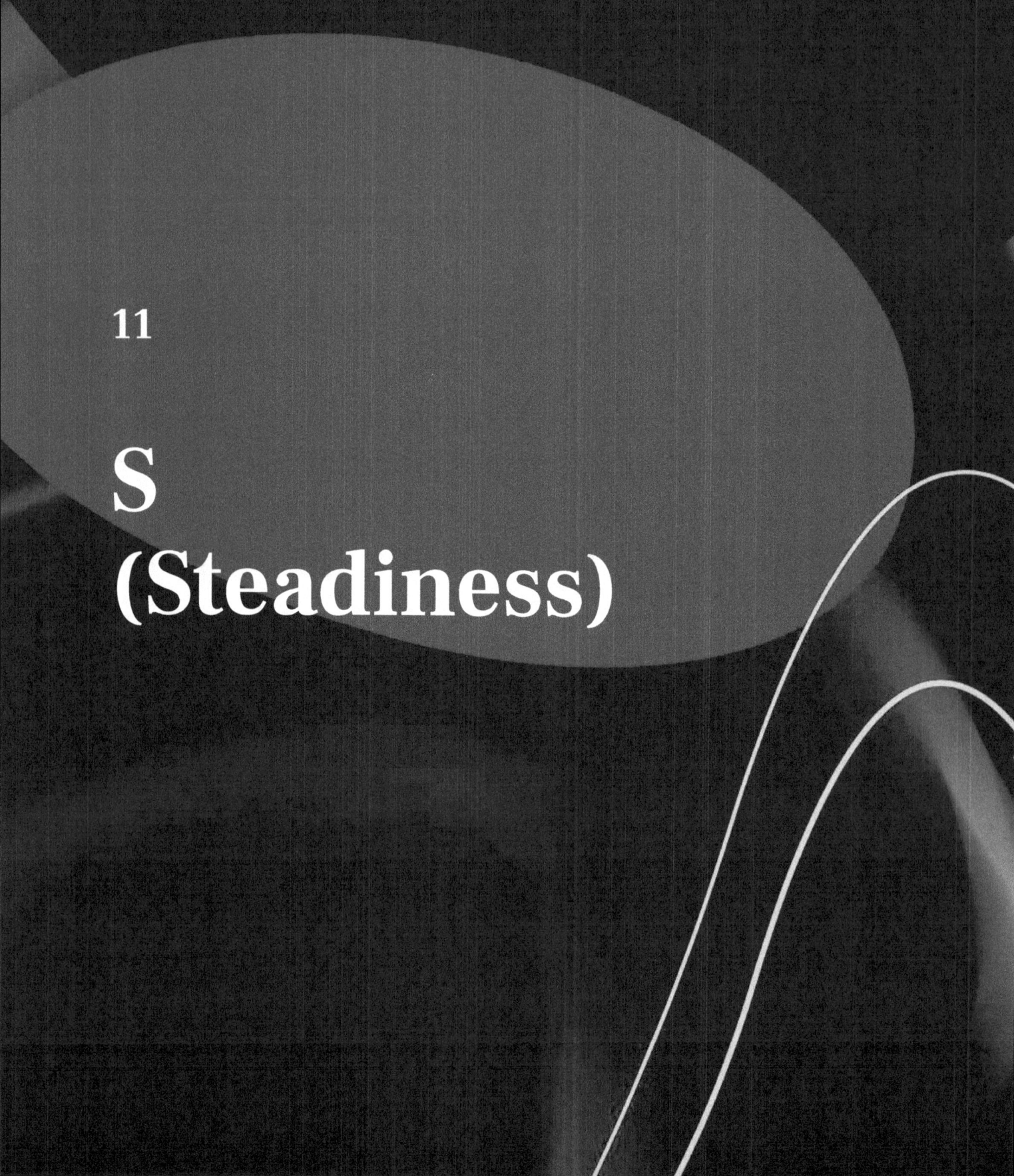

11

S
(Steadiness)

Desires:

- Stability and predictability in their environment
- Peaceful and supportive relationships
- Familiar routines and known expectations

Fears:

- Unexpected or abrupt changes
- Tensions or confrontational episodes
- Feeling uprooted or insecure

Communication Strategies:

- Approach with calmness, avoiding aggressive tones.
- Offer them ample time to process new information.
- Emphasize the familiar and provide consistent assurance.

Scenario: Introducing a new office software to Anna, an "S" type, might initially overwhelm her. By explaining the parallels between the new system and the old while assuring her of continuous support, Anna's transition can become smoother and more receptive.

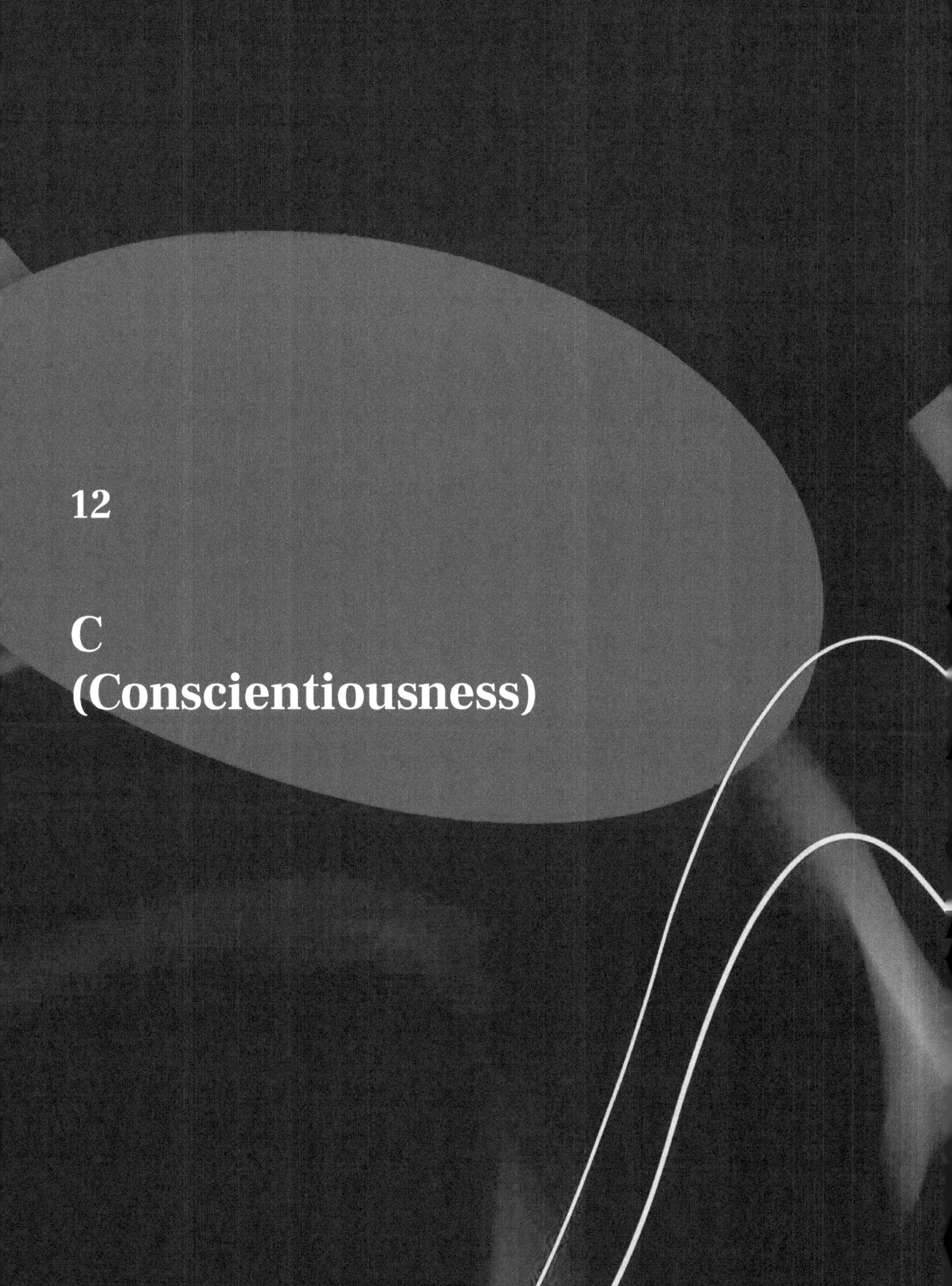

12

C
(Conscientiousness)

Desires:

- Accuracy and diligence in tasks
- Adherence to established norms
- Deep analytical challenges and problem-solving opportunities

Fears:

- Facing criticism for minor oversights
- Being labeled as inadequate
- Ambiguous instructions or undefined expectations

Communication Strategies:

- Provide exhaustive details and clear directives.
- Be patient, addressing their queries comprehensively.
- Applaud their meticulous nature and precision.

Scenario: When working with Alex, a "C" personality, on a data analysis project, ensure he can access all necessary data sets. Regular feedback sessions emphasizing accuracy and thoroughness will boost his confidence and productivity.

Comprehending each DISC personality type's unique motivations and concerns is instrumental for effective communication. By employing tailored approaches based on these insights, we can foster enriched relationships, enhance teamwork, and achieve organizational goals with greater synergy.

13

The Key to Dealing with Difficult People

Personality Type

Dominance (D) Type

Direct, decisive, strong-willed, and

They can become overly aggressive impatient, and might dominate

Be Direct: Address the issue head-on.

Stay Calm: Respond with a steady voice. Acknowledge Their Point: Show understanding. Provide Solutions: They value problem-solving.

Personality Type

Influence (I) Type

Outgoing, enthusiastic, optimistic, and likes collaborating with others.

Might become emotional, scattered, or seek validation from others.

Stay Positive: Maintain a positive

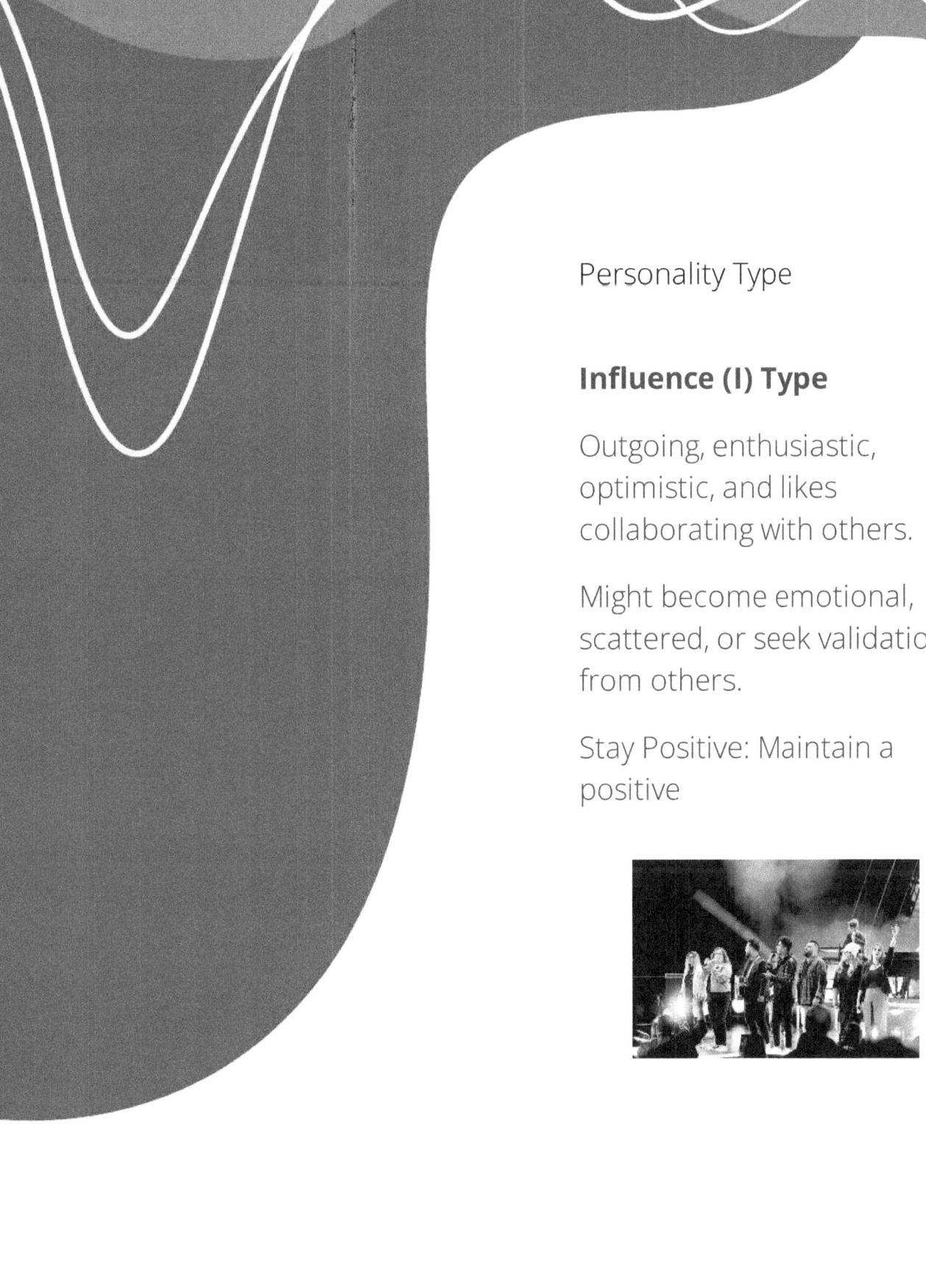

Personality Type

Steadiness (S) Type

Calm, patient, consistent, and values peace and

Might withdraw, avoid confrontation, or become passive-aggressive.

Create a Safe Space: Ensure comfort. Be Patient: Allow time to process. Ask Open-Ended Questions: Encourage sharing. Reiterate Stability: Emphasize consistency.

Conscientiousness (C) Type

Analytical, detail-oriented, systematic

Might become overly critical, withdraw, or focus excessively on minor details.

Be Detailed: Address with clarity. Acknowledge

Perspective: Value attention to detail. Avoid Being Vague: Offer clear answers. Request Feedback: Solicit solutions.

"Friends" is a beloved TV show. While its characters are fictional with multifaceted personalities, we can still attempt to categorize them into DISC styles based on their prevalent traits. Remember that real individuals (and even detailed fictional characters) can exhibit behaviors from multiple DISC categories. Here's an overview:

1. Rachel Green:

- Primary DISC Style: Influence (I)
- Rationale: Rachel is outgoing, enthusiastic, and friendly. While she thrives in social settings and often seeks validation, her increasing focus on her career across the seasons also hints at Dominance.

1. Monica Geller:

- Primary DISC Style: Conscientiousness (C)
- Rationale: Monica's detail-oriented nature is evident in her role as a chef and her penchant for cleanliness and order. Her analytical mindset values precision.

1. Ross Geller:

- Primary DISC Style: Conscientiousness (C)
- Rationale: As a paleontologist, Ross leans towards logic and detail. He prioritizes facts and accuracy and often approaches situations systematically. However, his relational traits also resonate with Steadiness.

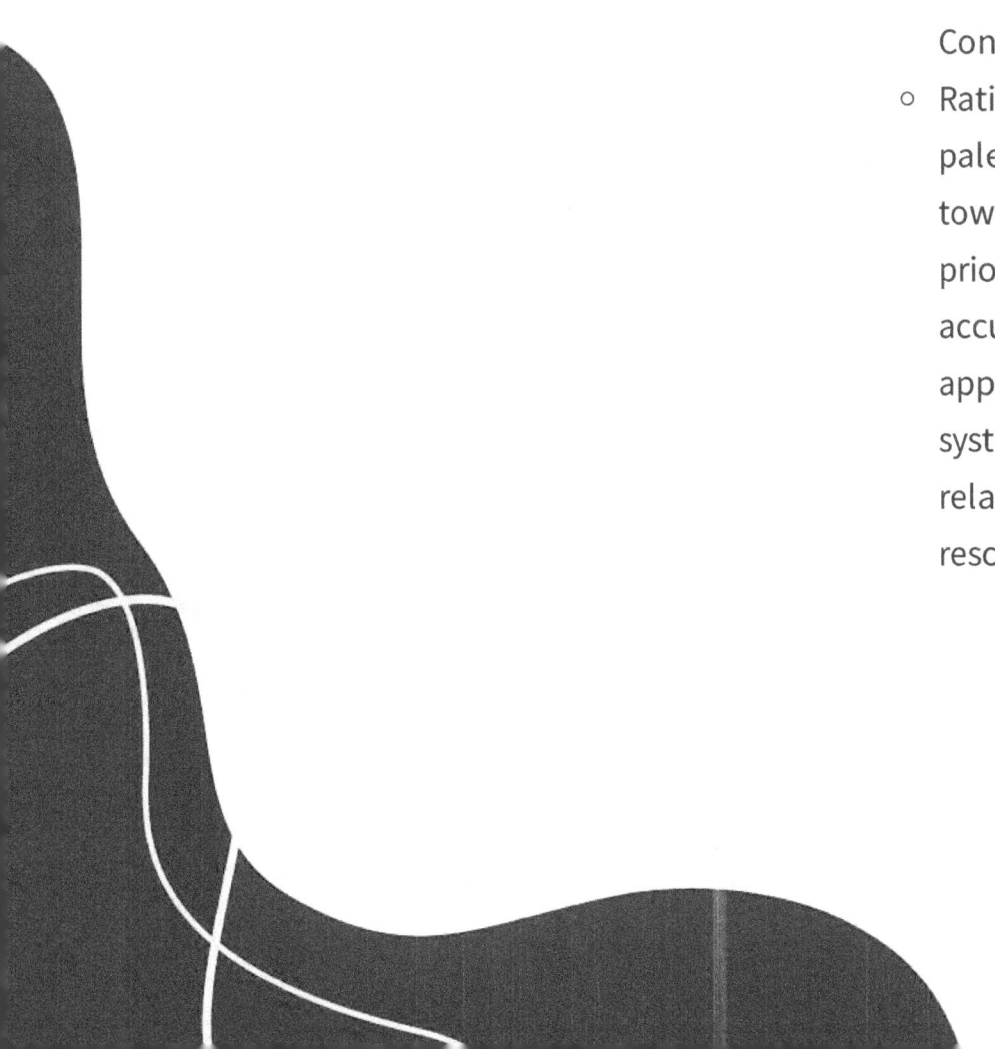

1. Chandler Bing:

- Primary DISC Style: Influence (I)
- Rationale: Chandler's humor, often a defense mechanism, places him in the spotlight during social interactions. His wit and charm navigate many situations.

It's worth noting that these assessments are based on a broad observation of each character's behaviors and traits throughout the series. Part of "Friends'" charm lies in its intricately designed characters who, much like real individuals, aren't easily confined to a single category.

-

- DISC personality types for U.S. presidents are quite speculative, as these individuals never took a DISC assessment (and the model wasn't even developed until the 1920s). However, we can make informed assumptions based on historical records, writings, behaviors, and actions.
- Here's a speculative table:

President Speculative DISC Personality Type Rationale Thomas Jefferson Influence (I) The principal author of the Declaration of Independence showcased his persuasive abilities. James Madison Steadiness (S) "Father of the Constitution" with a systematic and collaborative approach.

President	Speculative DISC Personality Type	Rationale
Gerald Ford	Steadiness (S)	Calm demeanor during the post-Watergate period.
Jimmy Carter	Influence (I)	Focus on human rights and post-presidential humanitarian efforts.
Ronald Reagan	Influence (I)	Charisma and communication skills.
George H.W. Bush	Steadiness (S)	Diplomatic and cautious approach to foreign policy.
Bill Clinton	Influence (I)	Ability to connect with people and charismatic nature.
George W. Bush	Dominance (D)	Assertive approach to the War on Terror.

President	Speculative DISC Personality Type	Rationale
Barack Obama	Influence (I)	Inspirational speeches and focus on healthcare reform.

President	Speculative DISC Personality Type	Rationale
Donald Trump	Dominance (D)	Assertive communication style and business background.
Joe Biden	Steadiness (S)	Long career in the Senate and emphasis on unity and bipartisanship.

14

Optimizing Communication by DISC Type

Communicating with Dominance (D) Types:

- Be Direct: D-types value clarity and conciseness. Be straightforward and omit unnecessary details.
- Focus on Results: Emphasize the main outcome or objective.

Example: "This change will boost our sales by 15%."

Interacting with Influence (I) Types:

- Engage Emotionally: I-types are sociable. Share a personal story or inquire about their recent activities.
- Be Enthusiastic: Mirror their energy and display genuine interest in the dialogue.

Scenario: At a company event, before diving into work-related topics with an I-type, begin with, "I heard you recently went hiking! How was it?"

Engaging with Steadiness (S) Types:

- Be Calm and Respectful: Steer clear of aggressive tones or abrupt shifts.
- Provide Assurance: Emphasize the importance of the relationship and offer regular feedback.

Example: "I truly appreciate our collaboration, and I'm confident this new venture will be equally successful."

Relating to Compliance (C) Types:

- Offer Details: C-types value thoroughness. Be prepared to present facts, figures, or references.
- Stay Structured: Maintain an organized conversation that follows a logical sequence.

Scenario: When reviewing a report with a C-type, present the document systematically, ensuring every aspect is addressed.

Tailoring Strategies for Daily Interactions

In Meetings: Observe attendees' non-verbal cues. If someone exhibits typical D-type impatience, expedite the discussion or emphasize outcomes. If someone poses numerous detailed queries, they might be a C-type.

In Social Settings: An individual actively participating in casual conversation and being the center of attention might be an I-type. Conversely, a serene, attentive listener could be an S-type.

In Written Communication: A brief, direct email comes from a D-type, while a comprehensive, organized email might suggest a C-type sender.

Interactive Engagement: As you read, reflect on your experiences. Have you encountered a classic D-type in your workplace? How do you think understanding DISC can change your relationships?

Further Reading: For those keen on delving deeper into the DISC methodology, [insert links or references to more in-depth resources on DISC].

Glossary:

- Dominance (D): Assertiveness, result-driven, challenge-oriented.
- Influence (I): Outgoing, enthusiastic, persuasive.
- Steadiness (S): Cooperative, patient, consistent.
- Compliance (C): Detail-oriented, logical, accurate.

Leveraging the DISC framework can significantly improve everyday communication. By customizing our approach to each personality, we can foster more robust and efficient connections in both personal and professional realms. The essence lies in observing, adapting, and reacting in a manner that aligns with the person's innate communication preference. With consistent application, the DISC technique can seamlessly integrate into our interactions, making each exchange more rewarding and harmonious.

15

Advanced Communication Skills for Leaders: A Transformational Workshop

Did you know?

93% of professionals believe enhanced communication skills can elevate their career trajectory. Dive into the realm of superior interactions, both personal and professional, with our meticulously crafted workshop.

Workshop Duration:

4 to 12 hours

Target Audience:

- Ambitious professionals eager to refine their communication.
- Managers and leaders desiring enriched team dynamics.

What Sets Us Apart?

Our unique blend of theoretical insights and hands-on activities, backed by real-world success stories, sets our workshop apart. We're not just teaching – we're transforming.

Objectives:

Upon completion, participants will:

1. Decode the art and science of effective communication.
2. Pinpoint their communication strengths and enhancement areas.
3. Master techniques that resonate in real-world scenarios.

Course Highlights:

- DISC Personality Assessments: Learn how to speak in the language that needs to be heard.
- Neuro-Linguistic Programming (NLP): Personal evolution through cognitive-behavioral approaches.
- Transformational Vocabulary: Words that change dialogues.
- Meta-Programs & AVK Styles: Subconscious shaping and sensory cues of communication.
- Emotional Intelligence: Building enriched interpersonal connections.
- Assertive Communication & Employee Coaching: Express, respect, guide, and mentor.

Interactive Elements: Our workshop thrives on engagement. Expect role-playing, group discussions, and problem-solving segments tailored to your real-life challenges.

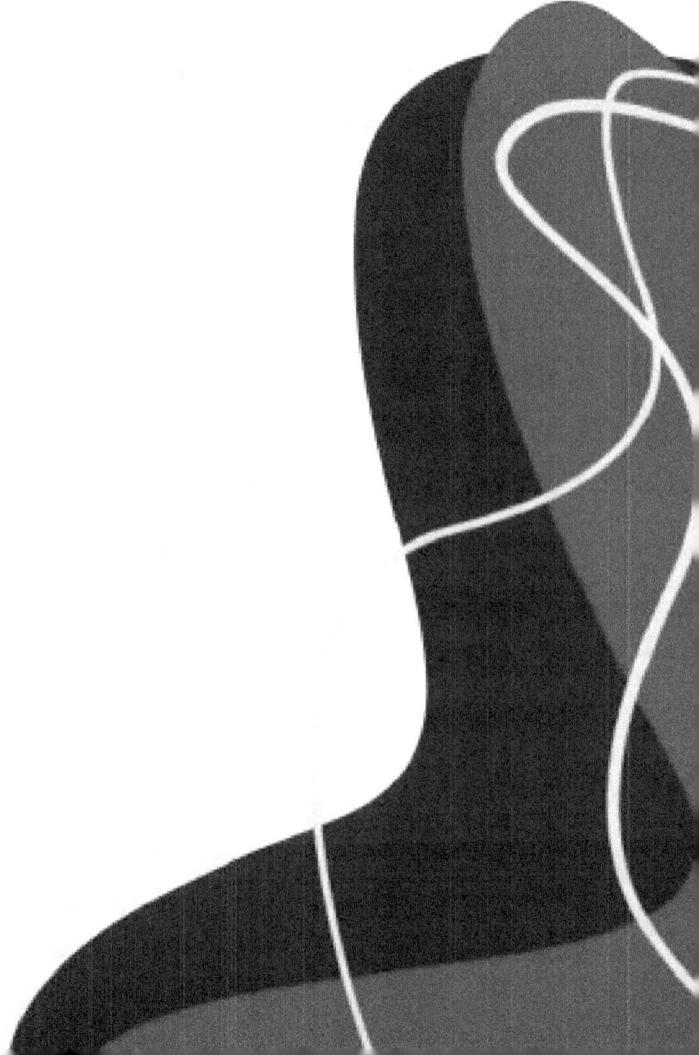

Methodology:

Beyond traditional lectures, we immerse participants in simulations and activities, ensuring they embody pivotal communication strategies.

Testimonials:

"This workshop transformed how we approach conversations at work. A must-do!" – Jane D., CEO

"I never realized the depth of communication until this workshop. Insightful and transformative." – Raj K., Team Leader

Benefits for Attendees:

1. Skill Augmentation: Navigate diverse conversational landscapes.
2. Boosted Confidence: Communicate with assertiveness and self-assurance.
3. Leadership Empowerment: Inspire and invigorate teams.

Post-Workshop Value:

We believe in ongoing growth. Attendees receive an exclusive resource pack, further reading for continued personal development, and access to our quarterly communication webinars.

Let's Discuss How We Can Transform Your Team's Communication!

Schedule a quick conversation at https://scheduleglenn.com to explore how we can redefine and enhance communication within your organization. Discover the potential benefits, group discounts, and early-bird offers that await you.